TIME FOR KIDS READERS

Visit

VANCOUVER

by Joy Dickerson

Harcourt

Orlando   Austin   Chicago   New York   Toronto   London   San Diego

Visit *The Learning Site!*
www.harcourtschool.com

BETWEEN *the* MOUNTAINS *and the* SEA

What's the best thing about Vancouver? People who live there have a hard time deciding. Is it the underwater adventure of the aquarium? How about the mysteries of the past at the Museum of Anthropology or the beautiful sights of Grouse Mountain? Or is it the city itself?

Bordered by the Grouse Mountains and the Fraser River, Vancouver is located in a beautiful natural setting.

Sitting between the mountains and the sea, Vancouver is a real mixture. It's a city, but the wilderness is very close. It's in North America, but it is home to many people from other parts of the world. Vancouver is in Canada, but the city rarely gets very cold.

Vancouver is in the Canadian province of British Columbia. That's just north of the state of Washington in the United States. The drive from Seattle, Washington, to Vancouver is only about three hours.

The Pacific Ocean forms a border of the city. In fact, Vancouver is Canada's largest Pacific port. The coastal range, a mountain range that runs north along the coast of British Columbia, forms another border. The Fraser River comes down out of the mountains and flows by downtown Vancouver.

MACKENZIE'S *Travels*

IT'S A FACT

THE NAME GAME

The island and the city of **VANCOUVER** are named for Captain George Vancouver, a British explorer who sailed along the Pacific coast in 1792.

THE FRASER RIVER is named for Simon Fraser. He built a string of fur trading posts in British Columbia.

THE STRAIT OF JUAN DE FUCA, believe it or not, is named after a Greek sailor, Apostolos Varianos. He explored the area in 1592. However, since he sailed for Spain, he decided to use a Spanish name, Juan de Fuca.

Alexander Mackenzie reached the Pacific Ocean by following the path of the Fraser River.

To travel from the Atlantic to the Pacific is a long journey today. It was even longer in 1793, when the only way to do it was by foot and by boat. That's when Alexander Mackenzie reached the place where the city of Vancouver now stands. He was the first European to cross British Columbia from east to west.

Mackenzie was born in Scotland, probably in 1764. He and his father left their home in the western isles of Scotland when Alexander was 10 years old. They arrived in New York City in time for the start of the American Revolution in 1776. To escape the war, the Mackenzies moved to Quebec.

When he was 15 years old, Alexander went to work for a company that traded food, cloth, and money to trappers for furs that could be sold in Europe. In 1789 Mackenzie started traveling west, looking for new markets for his company and, at the same time, a water route that would take him all the way to the Pacific Ocean.

Alexander Mackenzie at the Arctic Ocean

His first try to reach the Pacific, in 1789, was a failure. He ended up at the Arctic Ocean. The river he followed to get there is now named after him.

Mackenzie was not one to give up. He went to England to brush up on his navigation and map skills. In 1793, back in North America, Mackenzie set out again. In his large birch-bark canoe, he took with him two Native American guides; seven French, English, and Scottish fur traders; and his dog. This time, Mackenzie knew that he had to leave the river before it turned north to the Arctic.

The group followed many different rivers across the Rocky Mountains. The journey was challenging. After they lost their canoe, Mackenzie and his companions walked for two weeks, carrying all their gear. They followed the Fraser River down into British Columbia. On July 22, 1793, they reached the Pacific Ocean. Mackenzie was 29 years old. He had become the first person to find a way through the Rockies and to cross North America.

The story of his two westward journeys is told in the journal that Mackenzie kept and published in 1801. In his book he gave credit to his Native American guide, Nestabeck, for keeping him on the right trail.

Through all his adventures, Mackenzie always thought of Scotland as home. He returned there in 1812. He died in 1820.

Hundreds of boats are docked in Vancouver's harbor.

VANCOUVER
Surprises

Getting to Vancouver these days is a lot easier than it was in Mackenzie's time. Visitors today might see some of the same sights that he saw. For example, visitors to Vancouver may find the city's palm trees to be an unexpected sight. For, even though the city is in Canada, the weather is mild. It's never too hot or too cold. A warm-water current in the Pacific Ocean, the Japan Current, keeps temperatures from falling very low. In the winter, the temperature rarely sinks below 37°F (3°C). In the summer, the high temperature stays around 70°F (20°C).

The beautiful weather makes Vancouver an ideal spot for many activities. Its harbor stays open and free of ice year-round. In 1891 the *Empress of India* became the first ocean liner to arrive in Vancouver from Asia. Now ships from all over the world come there to load and unload cargo. British Columbia has vast forests, and lumber is one of its main exports. Much of this lumber leaves British Columbia from Vancouver's harbor.

The harbor is also an important stop for cruise ships. Vancouver is often the first and the last stop for these ships. Each year dozens of cruise ships, big and small, carry tourists though the waterways of the Alaskan panhandle. Tens of thousands of visitors pass through Vancouver every year on their way to Alaska. The tourists see the giant glaciers and the wildlife, such as bald eagles and grizzly bears. The ships stop at many islands along the way.

Moviegoers, especially, may see Vancouver all the time—even if they haven't actually been there. That's because Vancouver stands in for many United States cities on the big screen. Is that a neighborhood in Seattle? Or is it Vancouver? Is that a street in Chicago? Or is it Vancouver? That's New York for sure! Or . . . is it Vancouver? The weather is, of course, one reason that Vancouver has become a major moviemaking center. Its mild climate allows filming almost year-round. Does a director want waves crashing on a shore? In the Vancouver area, a crew can film at the ocean in the morning. By mid-afternoon, it can be filming skiing scenes at the top of a snow-capped mountain.

TEK 5

These movies were shot in Vancouver (while pretending to take place elsewhere):

Best In Show
Dudley Do Right
Josie & the Pussycats
Saving Silverman
Mission to Mars

Many United States movies are filmed in Vancouver.

ARTS & CRAFTS
and the
COAST SALISH

Many people visit Vancouver to learn about and enjoy the culture of the First Nations. First Nations and First Peoples are the Canadian names for the people who were living in North America when the European explorers arrived.

The people of the First Nations who lived in the Vancouver area, and who still live there today, belong to a group called the Coast Salish. The Nootka, Makah, Kwakiutl, and Chinook peoples lived nearby.

The art of Coast Salish people is among the first sights visitors see when they land at the Vancouver airport. Richly colored weaving decorates the terminal. The large cloths are made from hand-dyed yarn. The weaving was created by members of the Musqueam Nation, part of the Coast Salish. For thousands of years the Musqueam have lived in the place where Vancouver now stands. They still live on and own land in the city.

Totem poles that Musqueam artists carve are used to decorate places in Vancouver.

The Coast Salish, like some Native American tribes in the northwestern United States, lived in longhouses. Each village was made up of a small number of longhouses. The houses were often arranged in a half-circle or set in a long row. One extended family—a group of relatives—lived in each longhouse. It wasn't unusual for 30 or more members of the same family to live in one long longhouse.

The corner posts and door posts of each Musqueam longhouse were carefully carved. The Europeans, when they first saw these carvings, called them totem poles.

Guarded and decorated by tall totem poles, a copy of a longhouse that visitors can enter stands on the grounds of the Museum of Anthropology. First Nations artists are often at work at this longhouse. They are carving new totem poles to keep alive a very old art.

Totem pole carvings have many meanings. Some show a family's place in the community. Others record the history of a village or tell stories. The figures in the carvings are often animals. Wolves, bears, eagles, ravens, and frogs are favorite subjects. The carver of a totem pole wants the spirit of the wood to be able to breathe. So, most poles are not painted. Instead, stains are used to accent and highlight the wood's grain.

Vancouver and its surrounding areas are good places to see examples of totem poles. Some stand in Stanley Park. The Museum of Anthropology is also a great place to see examples of totem poles and learn more about the First Nations of Canada. The museum is part of the University of British Columbia, which has totem poles and masks carved by Coast Salish artists. A huge room of stately totem poles looks out over the waters of the Strait of Georgia.

Gastown is one of the liveliest sections of Vancouver.

getting to know
THE NEIGHBORS

Gastown is one of the oldest neighborhoods in Vancouver. It started out as an inn in 1867. The owner, Jack Deighton, talked so much that people called him "Gassy Jack." Soon, they were calling the settlement around Deighton's inn "Gastown." A city grew up around Gastown, and later Gastown's name was changed to Vancouver.

Gastown is famous for its old streets, which are paved with cobblestones. Here, shops and restaurants serve foods from all over the world. Tourists like to have their pictures taken in front of the world's first steam clock. It stands at the corner of Cambie and Water streets, where it whistles out music every 15 minutes.

Near Gastown is Chinatown, which is also packed with restaurants and shops, but with a Chinese flavor. That's because many of the people who live there are Chinese Canadians. Chinese people first came to Vancouver to work on the railroad. When work on the Great Northern Railway was completed in 1904, the workers stayed. Vancouver's Chinatown has the second-largest population of Chinese people in North America. (The largest community is in San Francisco.)

The Dr. Sun Yat-Sen Classical Chinese Garden is a main attraction of Chinatown. It honors the memory of one of China's most important leaders of the early 1900s. The garden, built in the style of traditional Ming dynasty gardens in China, is the only one of its kind outside of China. It is a beautiful place to rest and become refreshed.

A parade in Chinatown celebrates the heritage of its residents.

At 8 Pender Street in Chinatown is the Sam Kee Building, which is said to be the narrowest building in the world. It is only six feet (1.5 meters) from front to back. In 1913 the Sam Kee Company was angry at the city of Vancouver. City officials had refused to pay the company for land needed to widen Pender Street. To everyone's surprise, the company took its revenge by constructing the building on a little strip of land that the city didn't use.

Vancouver is an international city. On its streets, many different languages are spoken and the aromas hint of many different kinds of food. In addition to people from China and Japan, many people from India and Pakistan also make their home in the Vancouver area.

A DAY Out

Most people in Vancouver dress casually. Jeans and cowboy boots are seen often. Vancouver is known as a very polite city. The drivers here are famous for *not* honking. The sound of honking in Vancouver means there's a real emergency!

Wildlife is always close by in Vancouver. In fact, it's close to downtown, just a few miles from the business area. Coyotes and owls, along with dozens of other kinds of animals, live in Stanley Park. It covers more than 1,000 acres, and most of it is forest. It has miles of nature trails and a water park. Stanley Park is so large that it even has room for a miniature railroad, tennis courts, a children's farmyard, a cricket field (for cricket players), and a paved seaside path used by walkers, in-line skaters, and bike riders. A person might become very tired in Stanley Park, but never bored!

The Vancouver Aquarium is also in Stanley Park. Orcas and beluga whales make their home here, as do Amazon sloths, iguanas, and sea otters. Visitors can watch as the zookeepers swim with and feed the orcas. This keeps the animals in top shape and teaches humans about them at the same time. In another part of the aquarium, salmon swim upstream. In yet another area, a tropical rain forest comes complete with piranhas! Trailing fingers in the water is strictly forbidden here. The piranhas are fed well enough!

North American bald eagles can be seen in Vancouver Island, which is close to Vancouver.

The Parliament building is located in Victoria, Vancouver Island. The city is the capital of British Columbia.

ANOTHER VANCOUVER

About 20 miles (32 km) west of Vancouver is a large island, also called Vancouver. Vancouver Island is the biggest island on the west coast of North America. Victoria, the capital city of British Columbia, is at the southern tip of Vancouver Island. The Strait of Georgia separates the city from the island.

TFK
IT'S A FACT

Whale Radio

The Vancouver Aquarium has its own radio station. On 88.5 ORCA-FM, listen to free-swimming orcas singing all along the coast of British Columbia.

This beluga whale is one of the attractions at the Vancouver Aquarium.

It's clear that Vancouver is a city rich in culture, history, and natural features. Totem poles stand next to skyscrapers. Beaches are within two hours of the mountaintops. Best of all, it's a place where many different kinds of people live together in harmony. In other words, Vancouver is a wonderful place to live— and to visit!

Places to visit in
Vancouver

1. Grouse Mountain
2. Chinatown
3. Stanley Park
4. Gastown
5. Vancouver Aquarium

Grouse Mountain offers a spectacular view of Vancouver.